This Journal belongs to

_____

In Loving Memory of

_____

Healing my heart © 2022 - Melissa Desveaux

Published in Australia by Melissa Desveaux

All rights reserved. This book contains material protected under
international and Federal Copyright Laws and Treaties. Any unauthorized reprint or use of this material is prohibited. No part of this book/document may be reproduced or transmitted in any form or by any means - electronic, mechanical, photocopy, recording or otherwise, without written permission from the publisher.

Cover & interior design - Melissa Desveaux

Contact@melissadesveaux.com
www.Melissadesveaux.com

I'm Sorry for your Loss ♡

Nothing can ever take away the way you feel after experiencing the heartbreak of losing your baby.

This journal is one to help you navigate your way through your grief. You will find space inside to:

- Write your daily thoughts and feelings for 31 days

- Plan rituals to set you up for daily routines

- Create Healing Goals

- Practice poses for Meditation and Yoga

- Keep track of your Meditation

- Track your Self care routine

- Write personal notes, favourite memories, and inspirations

- Read Loving Quotes

- Write a letter to your baby

- Keep photos and special memories

- Get support

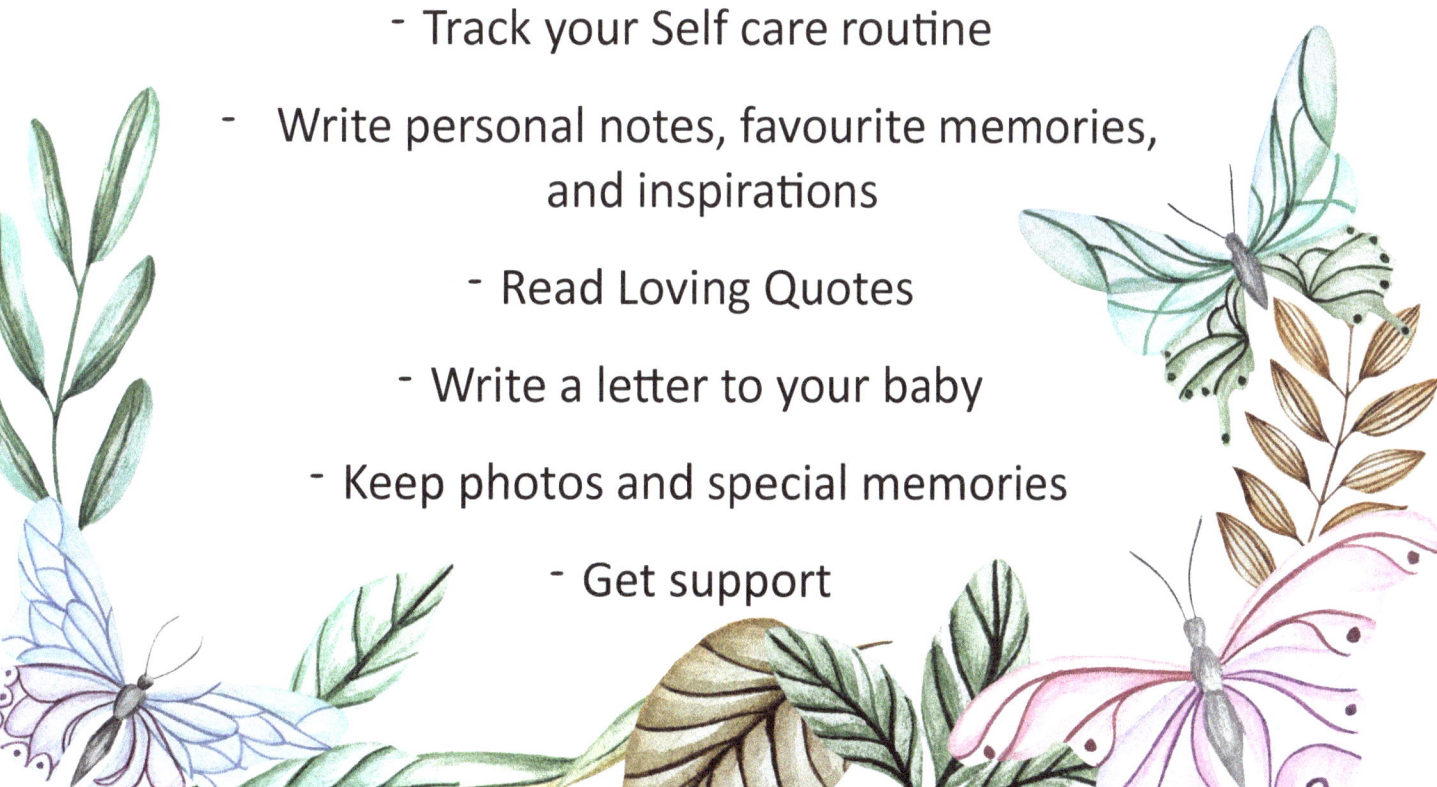

My Stages Of Grief ♡

Denial & Shock

Anger & Pain

Bargaining

Depression & Loneliness

Acknowledgment

Write down how you felt or are feeling as you experience each stage of grief

My Healing Goals 🖤

1. ....
2. ....
3. ....
4. ....
5. ....
6. ....
7. ....
8. ....
9. ....
10. ....
11. ....
12. ....
13. ....

What do you want to acheive as you heal?

Examples could be:

Safety

Calm and relaxed

Grounded

Simplicity

Security

Goodness

Full of life

Happiness

Change in mindset

Set boundaries

Have a support group

Self Care Suggestions ♡

Go for a walk

Play games

Exercise

Experience nature

Have a spa day

Go out for dinner

Rest

Watch a fun movie

Hug a loved one

Talk about your feelings

See a doctor or councellor

Meditate

Make something to donate

Write

Ask for help

Get creative

Read relatable stories

Listen to music

Self Care Log

Date :

Task	Done
	○
	○
	○
	○
	○
	○
	○
	○
	○
	○
	○
	○

Those we love don't go away They walk beside us every day ♥

Ritual Planner

Date :

Time	Place	Ritual	Notes

Survival Planner

Date :

The Worst That Could Happen

My Survival Plan

Meditation & Yoga Poses

Meditation can help you relieve stress and anxiety through deep breathing and mindfullness techniques to keep you calm and relaxed.

There are many apps you can download to your phone to guide you through meditation such as; Calm, Insight Timer, Smiling Mind, or Deep Relax.

These can be guided or purely relaxing sounds and music.

There are many variations of meditations so if you're just starting out, try using one of the guided apps.

The basic steps for meditation:

Sit in a comfortable and quiet place.

Close your eyes.

Take deep breaths in through your nose, hold for a few seconds and slowly breath out through your mouth.

Focus only on how your body is feeling, starting from your feet to the top of your head.

If you get side tracked, bring your focus back to your breathing. You can do this for as little as two minutes however aim for at least ten minutes daily.

See some meditation poses on the opposite page.

Yoga is a form of stretching and breathing exercise. There are numerous videos online for example, YouTube, you can watch for free in the comfort of your home or you can take a class at a local gym or studio where they teach it.

Yoga can help with clearing the mind by stretching different parts of your body, releasing tense muscles and balancing to keep you focused.

You can see some poses on the opposite page.

Meditation Log

Time	Method	Duration

Meditation Log

Date :

Time	Method	Duration

One Day at a Time

Date:

Today's Highlights

Feeling: 😃 🙂 😐 ☹️ 😖

Why I Feel This Way

Having A Hard Time With

Missing The Most :

Greatful For Today :

What Made Me Feel Better :

One Day at a Time

Date:

Today's Highlights

Feeling: 😃 🙂 😐 🙁 😖

Why I Feel This Way

Having A Hard Time With

Missing The Most :

Greatful For Today :

What Made Me Feel Better :

One Day at a Time

Date :

Today's Highlights

Feeling :

Why I Feel This Way

Having A Hard Time With

Missing The Most :

Greatful For Today :

What Made Me Feel Better :

One Day at a Time ♡

Date :

Today's Highlights

Feeling : 😃 🙂 😐 🙁 😖

Why I Feel This Way

Having A Hard Time With

Missing The Most :

Greatful For Today :

What Made Me Feel Better :

One Day at a Time ♡ Date:

Today's Highlights

Feeling: 😀 🙂 😐 🙁 😣

Why I Feel This Way

Having A Hard Time With

Missing The Most :

Greatful For Today :

What Made Me Feel Better :

One Day at a Time ♡ Date:

Today's Highlights

Feeling : 😀 ☺ 😐 ☹ 😖

Why I Feel This Way

Having A Hard Time With

Missing The Most :

Greatful For Today :

What Made Me Feel Better :

One Day at a Time ♡

Date:

Today's Highlights

Feeling : 😀 ☺ 😐 ☹ 😣

Why I Feel This Way

Having A Hard Time With

Missing The Most :

Greatful For Today :

What Made Me Feel Better :

One Day at a Time ♡

Date :

Today's Highlights

Feeling : 😀 ☺ 😐 ☹ 😣

Why I Feel This Way

Having A Hard Time With

Missing The Most :

Greatful For Today :

What Made Me Feel Better :

One Day at a Time ♡

Date:

Today's Highlights

Feeling : 😃 🙂 😐 🙁 😣

Why I Feel This Way

Having A Hard Time With

Missing The Most :

Greatful For Today :

What Made Me Feel Better :

One Day at a Time ♡

Date :

Today's Highlights

Feeling : 😃 ☺ 😐 ☹ 😣

Why I Feel This Way

Having A Hard Time With

Missing The Most :

Greatful For Today :

What Made Me Feel Better :

One Day at a Time ♡

Date:

Today's Highlights

Feeling: 😃 🙂 😐 🙁 😣

Why I Feel This Way

Having A Hard Time With

Missing The Most:

Greatful For Today:

What Made Me Feel Better:

One Day at a Time ♡ Date :

Today's Highlights

Feeling : 😀 🙂 😐 🙁 😖

Why I Feel This Way

Having A Hard Time With

Missing The Most :

Greatful For Today :

What Made Me Feel Better :

One Day at a Time

Date :

Today's Highlights

Feeling : 😃 ☺ 😐 ☹ 😖

Why I Feel This Way

Having A Hard Time With

Missing The Most :

Greatful For Today :

What Made Me Feel Better :

One Day at a Time

Date :

Today's Highlights

Feeling :

Why I Feel This Way

Having A Hard Time With

Missing The Most :

Greatful For Today :

What Made Me Feel Better :

One Day at a Time ♡

Date :

Today's Highlights

Feeling : 😃 🙂 😐 🙁 😣

Why I Feel This Way

Having A Hard Time With

Missing The Most :

Greatful For Today :

What Made Me Feel Better :

One Day at a Time ♡ Date:

Today's Highlights

Feeling: 😀 🙂 😐 🙁 😣

Why I Feel This Way

Having A Hard Time With

Missing The Most :

Greatful For Today :

What Made Me Feel Better :

One Day at a Time

Date:

Today's Highlights

Feeling:

Why I Feel This Way

Having A Hard Time With

Missing The Most :

Greatful For Today :

What Made Me Feel Better :

One Day at a Time ♡

Date :

Today's Highlights

Feeling : 😃 🙂 😐 🙁 😣

Why I Feel This Way

Having A Hard Time With

Missing The Most :

Greatful For Today :

What Made Me Feel Better :

One Day at a Time ♡ Date:

Today's Highlights

Feeling : 😃 🙂 😐 🙁 😣

Why I Feel This Way

Having A Hard Time With

Missing The Most :

Greatful For Today :

What Made Me Feel Better :

One Day at a Time

Date:

Today's Highlights

Feeling: 😃 🙂 😐 🙁 😣

Why I Feel This Way

Having A Hard Time With

Missing The Most:

Greatful For Today:

What Made Me Feel Better:

One Day at a Time

Date :

Today's Highlights

Feeling : 😃   🙂   😐   🙁   😖

Why I Feel This Way

Having A Hard Time With

Missing The Most :

Greatful For Today :

What Made Me Feel Better :

One Day at a Time ♡

Date :

Today's Highlights

Feeling : 😀 🙂 😐 🙁 😣

Why I Feel This Way

Having A Hard Time With

Missing The Most :

Greatful For Today :

What Made Me Feel Better :

One Day at a Time ♡

Date :

Today's Highlights

Feeling : 😀 🙂 😐 🙁 😣

Why I Feel This Way

Having A Hard Time With

Missing The Most :

Greatful For Today :

What Made Me Feel Better :

One Day at a Time ♥ Date:

Today's Highlights

Feeling: 😃 🙂 😐 🙁 😣

Why I Feel This Way

Having A Hard Time With

Missing The Most :

Greatful For Today :

What Made Me Feel Better :

One Day at a Time

Date:

Today's Highlights

Feeling: 😀   🙂   😐   🙁   😖

Why I Feel This Way

Having A Hard Time With

Missing The Most :

Greatful For Today :

What Made Me Feel Better :

One Day at a Time

Date :

Today's Highlights

Feeling :

Why I Feel This Way

Having A Hard Time With

Missing The Most :

Greatful For Today :

What Made Me Feel Better :

One Day at a Time

Date:

Today's Highlights

Feeling: 😃 ☺ 😐 ☹ 😣

Why I Feel This Way

Having A Hard Time With

Missing The Most :

Greatful For Today :

What Made Me Feel Better :

One Day at a Time

Date:

Today's Highlights

Feeling: 😃 🙂 😐 🙁 😣

Why I Feel This Way

Having A Hard Time With

Missing The Most :

Greatful For Today :

What Made Me Feel Better :

One Day at a Time

Date:

Today's Highlights

Feeling:

Why I Feel This Way

Having A Hard Time With

Missing The Most :

Greatful For Today :

What Made Me Feel Better :

One Day at a Time

Date:

Today's Highlights

Feeling:

Why I Feel This Way

Having A Hard Time With

Missing The Most :

Greatful For Today :

What Made Me Feel Better :

One Day at a Time ♡ Date:

Today's Highlights

Feeling: 😀 🙂 😐 🙁 😖

Why I Feel This Way

Having A Hard Time With

Missing The Most :

Greatful For Today :

What Made Me Feel Better :

Check in with yourself

How do you feel now?

Activities ♡

Date :

At Home

Outside

When someone you love becomes a memory
The memory becomes a treasure

My Inspirations

Date :

"
"

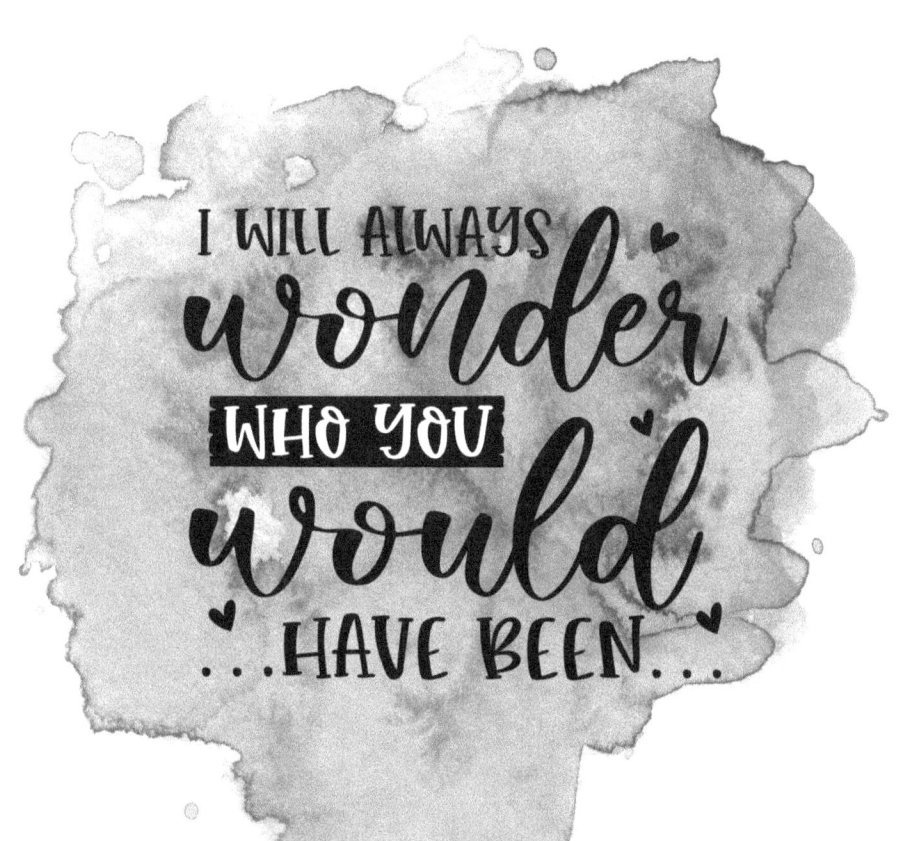

My Favorite Memories ♡

If love could have saved you You would have lived forever

Letter to my baby ♡

*On angels wings
you were taken away
But in my heart
you will always stay*

Letter to me ♡

Where there is great grief, there was great love

No matter what age your baby existed THEY MATTERED

Find Support

These organisations support families who have experienced pregnancy and infant loss.
Reach out to them if you feel you need additional support and someone to talk to.

- Aleisha' Angels
- Angel Gowns Australia
- Angels In Heaven
- Bears of Hope
- Beyond Blue
- Brother Bears
- Daily Strength Organization
- Empty Arms - Bereavement Support
- Exhale - Pro-Voice
- First Candle- peer-to-peer online support groups
- Gidget Foundation
- Guiding light
- Heartfelt
- Hope Mommies
- Kicks Count
- Lifeline
- Lullaby Trust
- March of Dimes
- Mater Mothers
- M.E.N.D. - Mommies Enduring Neonatal Death
- MISS Foundation
- Our Angel Bears
- PANDA - Perinatal, Anxiety & Depression Australia
- PSANZ - Perinatal Society - AU NZ
- Pillars of strength (support for bereaved fathers)
- Pink Elephants Support Network
- Postpartum Support International (PSI)
- Pregnancy Loss Australia
- Rednose
- Return to Zero Hope
- River's Gift
- SANDS - Stillborn and Newborn Death Support
- Saying Goodbye
- Sharing Solace
- Star Legacy Foundation
- Stillaware

Stillbirth Australia

Stillborn and Infant Loss - (SAILS)

The compassionate friends

The Miscarriage Association

The Stillbirth Foundation

The Tears Foundation

The Teddy Foundation

Tommy's Baby Loss Support

Walk with Me

WILMA - Womens Health Care Centre

Other support resources

Local hospital & GP

Libraries

Reach out to other parents

Write and share your story

Obstetrician

Family and friends

Read other stories about pregnancy & infant loss

Practice self-care

Support Groups on Facebook

Create your own community

Donate & fundraise for support organizations

Meditate or Pray

See a social worker/councellor

Make something for hospitals or organizations

Journal your thoughts and feelings

Thank you for purchasing this journal and I hope it brings you much comfort while you navigate your baby loss journey.

A portion of the profits received from the sale of this journal will be used to donate the book called *Letters of Love - Written for Pregnancy & Infant Loss,* to hospitals, libraries and other support organisations.

You can find a collection of my books and journals by visiting www.melissadesveaux.com/books.

With Love and Gratitude
Melissa